Case Brief Book

Course:

_____

Semester:

_____

Professor:

_____

Case Name

Page

Case Name

Page

Case Name

Page

Case Name	Page

Case: _____   Court: _____

Facts: _____
_____
_____
_____
_____

Issue: _____
_____
_____

Rule: _____
_____
_____

Analysis: _____
_____
_____
_____
_____
_____
_____
_____
_____
_____
_____

Conclusion/Holding: _____
_____
_____
_____

Vocab:	Questions:	☐ Upheld
		☐ Overturned
		☐ Questioned

Case: _____   Court: _____

Facts: _____
_____
_____
_____
_____

Issue: _____
_____
_____

Rule: _____
_____
_____

Analysis: _____
_____
_____
_____
_____
_____
_____
_____
_____
_____
_____
_____

Conclusion/Holding: _____
_____
_____
_____
_____

Vocab:	Questions:

☐ Upheld

☐ Overturned

☐ Questioned

Case: _____   Court: _____

Facts:
_____
_____
_____
_____
_____

Issue:
_____
_____
_____

Rule:
_____
_____
_____

Analysis:
_____
_____
_____
_____
_____
_____
_____
_____
_____
_____
_____
_____

Conclusion/Holding:
_____
_____
_____
_____

Vocab:	Questions:

☐ Upheld

☐ Overturned

☐ Questioned

Case: _____   Court: _____

Facts: _____
_____
_____
_____
_____

Issue: _____
_____
_____

Rule: _____
_____
_____

Analysis: _____
_____
_____
_____
_____
_____
_____
_____
_____
_____
_____
_____

Conclusion/Holding: _____
_____
_____
_____
_____

Vocab:	Questions:	
		☐ Upheld
		☐ Overturned
		☐ Questioned

Case: _____ Court: _____

Facts:
_____
_____
_____
_____
_____

Issue:
_____
_____

Rule:
_____
_____

Analysis:
_____
_____
_____
_____
_____
_____
_____
_____
_____
_____
_____

Conclusion/Holding:
_____
_____
_____
_____

Vocab:	Questions:	☐ Upheld
		☐ Overturned
		☐ Questioned

Case: _____   Court: _____

Facts: _____
_____
_____
_____
_____

Issue: _____
_____
_____

Rule: _____
_____
_____

Analysis: _____
_____
_____
_____
_____
_____
_____
_____
_____
_____
_____
_____

Conclusion/Holding: _____
_____
_____
_____
_____

Vocab:	Questions:	☐ Upheld
		☐ Overturned
		☐ Questioned

Case: _____ Court: _____

Facts: _____
_____
_____
_____
_____

Issue: _____
_____
_____

Rule: _____
_____
_____

Analysis: _____
_____
_____
_____
_____
_____
_____
_____
_____
_____
_____
_____

Conclusion/Holding: _____
_____
_____
_____
_____

Vocab:	Questions:	☐ Upheld
		☐ Overturned
		☐ Questioned

Case: _____ Court: _____

Facts:
_____
_____
_____
_____

Issue:
_____
_____

Rule:
_____
_____

Analysis:
_____
_____
_____
_____
_____
_____
_____
_____
_____
_____
_____

Conclusion/Holding:
_____
_____
_____
_____

Vocab:	Questions:	☐ Upheld
		☐ Overturned
		☐ Questioned

Case: _____   Court: _____

Facts: _____
_____
_____
_____

Issue: _____
_____

Rule: _____
_____
_____

Analysis: _____
_____
_____
_____
_____
_____
_____
_____
_____
_____
_____

Conclusion/Holding: _____
_____
_____
_____

Vocab:	Questions:	☐ Upheld
		☐ Overturned
		☐ Questioned

Case: _____ Court: _____

Facts:
_____
_____
_____
_____

Issue:
_____
_____

Rule:
_____
_____

Analysis:
_____
_____
_____
_____
_____
_____
_____
_____
_____
_____
_____

Conclusion/Holding:
_____
_____
_____
_____

Vocab:	Questions:	
		☐ Upheld
		☐ Overturned
		☐ Questioned

Case: _____   Court: _____

Facts: _____
_____
_____
_____
_____

Issue: _____
_____
_____

Rule: _____
_____
_____

Analysis: _____
_____
_____
_____
_____
_____
_____
_____
_____
_____
_____
_____

Conclusion/Holding: _____
_____
_____
_____
_____

Vocab:	Questions:	☐ Upheld
		☐ Overturned
		☐ Questioned

Case: _____ Court: _____

Facts:

_____

_____

_____

_____

Issue:

_____

_____

Rule:

_____

_____

Analysis:

_____

_____

_____

_____

_____

_____

_____

_____

_____

_____

_____

Conclusion/Holding:

_____

_____

_____

_____

Vocab:	Questions:	☐ Upheld
		☐ Overturned
		☐ Questioned

Case: _____ Court: _____

Facts: _____
_____
_____
_____
_____

Issue: _____
_____
_____

Rule: _____
_____
_____

Analysis: _____
_____
_____
_____
_____
_____
_____
_____
_____
_____
_____
_____
_____

Conclusion/Holding: _____
_____
_____
_____
_____

Vocab:	Questions:	☐ Upheld
		☐ Overturned
		☐ Questioned

Case: _____ Court: _____

Facts:
_____
_____
_____
_____
_____

Issue:
_____
_____

Rule:
_____
_____

Analysis:
_____
_____
_____
_____
_____
_____
_____
_____
_____
_____
_____

Conclusion/Holding:
_____
_____
_____
_____

Vocab:	Questions:	☐ Upheld
		☐ Overturned
		☐ Questioned

Case: _____ Court: _____

Facts: _____
_____
_____
_____
_____

Issue: _____
_____
_____

Rule: _____
_____
_____

Analysis: _____
_____
_____
_____
_____
_____
_____
_____
_____
_____
_____
_____

Conclusion/Holding: _____
_____
_____
_____
_____

Vocab:	Questions:	☐ Upheld
		☐ Overturned
		☐ Questioned

Case: _____ Court: _____

Facts: _____
_____
_____
_____
_____

Issue: _____
_____
_____

Rule: _____
_____
_____

Analysis: _____
_____
_____
_____
_____
_____
_____
_____
_____
_____
_____
_____
_____

Conclusion/Holding: _____
_____
_____
_____
_____

Vocab:	Questions:	☐ Upheld
		☐ Overturned
		☐ Questioned

Case: _____ Court: _____

Facts:
_____
_____
_____
_____
_____

Issue:
_____
_____

Rule:
_____
_____

Analysis:
_____
_____
_____
_____
_____
_____
_____
_____
_____
_____
_____

Conclusion/Holding:
_____
_____
_____
_____

Vocab:	Questions:	☐ Upheld
		☐ Overturned
		☐ Questioned

Case: _____ Court: _____

Facts: _____
_____
_____
_____
_____

Issue: _____
_____
_____

Rule: _____
_____
_____

Analysis: _____
_____
_____
_____
_____
_____
_____
_____
_____
_____
_____

Conclusion/Holding: _____
_____
_____
_____
_____

Vocab:	Questions:	
		☐ Upheld
		☐ Overturned
		☐ Questioned

Case: _____ Court: _____

Facts: _____
_____
_____
_____
_____

Issue: _____
_____

Rule: _____
_____
_____

Analysis: _____
_____
_____
_____
_____
_____
_____
_____
_____
_____
_____
_____

Conclusion/Holding: _____
_____
_____
_____
_____

Vocab:	Questions:	☐ Upheld
		☐ Overturned
		☐ Questioned

Case: _____ Court: _____

Facts:
_____
_____
_____
_____

Issue:
_____
_____

Rule:
_____
_____

Analysis:
_____
_____
_____
_____
_____
_____
_____
_____
_____
_____

Conclusion/Holding:
_____
_____
_____
_____

Vocab:	Questions:	☐ Upheld
		☐ Overturned
		☐ Questioned

Case: _____ Court: _____

Facts:
_____
_____
_____
_____
_____

Issue:
_____
_____

Rule:
_____
_____

Analysis:
_____
_____
_____
_____
_____
_____
_____
_____
_____
_____
_____

Conclusion/Holding:
_____
_____
_____
_____

Vocab:	Questions:	
		☐ Upheld
		☐ Overturned
		☐ Questioned

Case: _____ Court: _____

Facts: _____
_____
_____
_____

Issue: _____
_____

Rule: _____
_____

Analysis: _____
_____
_____
_____
_____
_____
_____
_____
_____
_____
_____

Conclusion/Holding: _____
_____
_____
_____

Vocab:	Questions:	☐ Upheld
		☐ Overturned
		☐ Questioned

Case: _____ Court: _____

Facts:
_____
_____
_____
_____
_____

Issue:
_____
_____

Rule:
_____
_____
_____

Analysis:
_____
_____
_____
_____
_____
_____
_____
_____
_____
_____
_____

Conclusion/Holding:
_____
_____
_____
_____

Vocab:	Questions:	☐ Upheld
		☐ Overturned
		☐ Questioned

Case: _____ Court: _____

Facts: _____
_____
_____
_____
_____

Issue: _____
_____

Rule: _____
_____
_____

Analysis: _____
_____
_____
_____
_____
_____
_____
_____
_____
_____
_____

Conclusion/Holding: _____
_____
_____
_____
_____

Vocab:	Questions:	☐ Upheld
		☐ Overturned
		☐ Questioned

Case: _____ Court: _____

Facts: _____
_____
_____
_____
_____

Issue: _____
_____

Rule: _____
_____

Analysis: _____
_____
_____
_____
_____
_____
_____
_____
_____
_____
_____

Conclusion/Holding: _____
_____
_____
_____
_____

Vocab:	Questions:	☐ Upheld
		☐ Overturned
		☐ Questioned

Case: _____ Court: _____

Facts:
_____
_____
_____
_____
_____

Issue:
_____
_____

Rule:
_____
_____

Analysis:
_____
_____
_____
_____
_____
_____
_____
_____
_____
_____
_____

Conclusion/Holding:
_____
_____
_____
_____

Vocab:	Questions:	
		☐ Upheld
		☐ Overturned
		☐ Questioned

57

Case: _____ Court: _____

Facts: _____
_____
_____
_____
_____

Issue: _____
_____
_____

Rule: _____
_____
_____

Analysis: _____
_____
_____
_____
_____
_____
_____
_____
_____
_____
_____
_____

Conclusion/Holding: _____
_____
_____
_____

Vocab:	Questions:	☐ Upheld
		☐ Overturned
		☐ Questioned

Case: _____ Court: _____

Facts: _____
_____
_____
_____
_____

Issue: _____
_____
_____

Rule: _____
_____
_____

Analysis: _____
_____
_____
_____
_____
_____
_____
_____
_____
_____
_____
_____

Conclusion/Holding: _____
_____
_____
_____
_____

Vocab:	Questions:	☐ Upheld
		☐ Overturned
		☐ Questioned

Case: _____ Court: _____

Facts: _____
_____
_____
_____
_____

Issue: _____
_____
_____

Rule: _____
_____
_____

Analysis: _____
_____
_____
_____
_____
_____
_____
_____
_____
_____
_____
_____

Conclusion/Holding: _____
_____
_____
_____
_____

Vocab:	Questions:	
		☐ Upheld
		☐ Overturned
		☐ Questioned

Case: _____   Court: _____

Facts: _____
_____
_____
_____
_____

Issue: _____
_____
_____

Rule: _____
_____
_____

Analysis: _____
_____
_____
_____
_____
_____
_____
_____
_____
_____
_____

Conclusion/Holding: _____
_____
_____
_____
_____

Vocab:	Questions:	☐ Upheld
		☐ Overturned
		☐ Questioned

Case: _____ Court: _____

Facts:
_____
_____
_____
_____
_____

Issue:
_____
_____

Rule:
_____
_____

Analysis:
_____
_____
_____
_____
_____
_____
_____
_____
_____
_____
_____

Conclusion/Holding:
_____
_____
_____
_____

Vocab:	Questions:	
		☐ Upheld
		☐ Overturned
		☐ Questioned

Case: _____   Court: _____

Facts:
_____
_____
_____
_____
_____

Issue:
_____
_____

Rule:
_____
_____

Analysis:
_____
_____
_____
_____
_____
_____
_____
_____
_____
_____

Conclusion/Holding:
_____
_____
_____
_____

Vocab:	Questions:	☐ Upheld
		☐ Overturned
		☐ Questioned

Case: _____ Court: _____

Facts: _____
_____
_____
_____
_____

Issue: _____
_____

Rule: _____
_____
_____

Analysis: _____
_____
_____
_____
_____
_____
_____
_____
_____
_____
_____
_____

Conclusion/Holding: _____
_____
_____
_____
_____

Vocab:	Questions:	☐ Upheld
		☐ Overturned
		☐ Questioned

Case: _____ Court: _____

Facts: _____
_____
_____
_____

Issue: _____
_____

Rule: _____
_____

Analysis: _____
_____
_____
_____
_____
_____
_____
_____
_____
_____
_____

Conclusion/Holding: _____
_____
_____
_____

Vocab:	Questions:	☐ Upheld
		☐ Overturned
		☐ Questioned

Case: _____   Court: _____

Facts: _____
_____
_____
_____
_____

Issue: _____
_____
_____

Rule: _____
_____
_____

Analysis: _____
_____
_____
_____
_____
_____
_____
_____
_____
_____
_____
_____

Conclusion/Holding: _____
_____
_____
_____
_____

Vocab:	Questions:

☐ Upheld

☐ Overturned

☐ Questioned

Case: _____ Court: _____

Facts: _____
_____
_____
_____
_____

Issue: _____
_____
_____

Rule: _____
_____
_____

Analysis: _____
_____
_____
_____
_____
_____
_____
_____
_____
_____
_____
_____
_____

Conclusion/Holding: _____
_____
_____
_____
_____

Vocab:	Questions:	
		☐ Upheld
		☐ Overturned
		☐ Questioned

Case: _____   Court: _____

Facts: _____
_____
_____
_____
_____

Issue: _____
_____

Rule: _____
_____
_____

Analysis: _____
_____
_____
_____
_____
_____
_____
_____
_____
_____
_____
_____

Conclusion/Holding: _____
_____
_____
_____
_____

Vocab:	Questions:	☐ Upheld
		☐ Overturned
		☐ Questioned

Case: _____ Court: _____

Facts: _____
_____
_____
_____
_____

Issue: _____
_____

Rule: _____
_____
_____

Analysis: _____
_____
_____
_____
_____
_____
_____
_____
_____
_____
_____

Conclusion/Holding: _____
_____
_____
_____
_____

Vocab:	Questions:	☐ Upheld
		☐ Overturned
		☐ Questioned

Case: _____ Court: _____

Facts: _____
_____
_____
_____
_____

Issue: _____
_____
_____

Rule: _____
_____
_____

Analysis: _____
_____
_____
_____
_____
_____
_____
_____
_____
_____
_____
_____

Conclusion/Holding: _____
_____
_____
_____

Vocab:	Questions:	☐ Upheld
		☐ Overturned
		☐ Questioned

Case: _____ Court: _____

Facts: _____
_____
_____
_____
_____

Issue: _____
_____
_____

Rule: _____
_____
_____

Analysis: _____
_____
_____
_____
_____
_____
_____
_____
_____
_____
_____

Conclusion/Holding: _____
_____
_____
_____
_____

Vocab:	Questions:	
		☐ Upheld
		☐ Overturned
		☐ Questioned

Case: _____ Court: _____

Facts:
_____
_____
_____
_____
_____

Issue:
_____
_____

Rule:
_____
_____

Analysis:
_____
_____
_____
_____
_____
_____
_____
_____
_____
_____
_____

Conclusion/Holding:
_____
_____
_____
_____

Vocab:	Questions:	
		☐ Upheld
		☐ Overturned
		☐ Questioned

Case: _____ Court: _____

Facts:
_____
_____
_____
_____
_____

Issue:
_____
_____

Rule:
_____
_____

Analysis:
_____
_____
_____
_____
_____
_____
_____
_____
_____
_____
_____

Conclusion/Holding:
_____
_____
_____
_____

Vocab:	Questions:	☐ Upheld
		☐ Overturned
		☐ Questioned

Case: _____   Court: _____

Facts: _____
_____
_____
_____
_____

Issue: _____
_____

Rule: _____
_____
_____

Analysis: _____
_____
_____
_____
_____
_____
_____
_____
_____
_____
_____

Conclusion/Holding: _____
_____
_____
_____
_____

Vocab:	Questions:

☐ Upheld

☐ Overturned

☐ Questioned

Case: _____ Court: _____

Facts:
_____
_____
_____
_____

Issue:
_____
_____

Rule:
_____
_____

Analysis:
_____
_____
_____
_____
_____
_____
_____
_____
_____
_____

Conclusion/Holding:
_____
_____
_____
_____

Vocab:	Questions:	☐ Upheld
		☐ Overturned
		☐ Questioned

Case: _____ Court: _____

Facts: _____
_____
_____
_____
_____

Issue: _____
_____
_____

Rule: _____
_____
_____

Analysis: _____
_____
_____
_____
_____
_____
_____
_____
_____
_____
_____
_____

Conclusion/Holding: _____
_____
_____
_____
_____

Vocab:	Questions:	
		☐ Upheld
		☐ Overturned
		☐ Questioned

95

Case: _____   Court: _____

Facts: _____
_____
_____
_____

Issue: _____
_____

Rule: _____
_____

Analysis: _____
_____
_____
_____
_____
_____
_____
_____
_____
_____
_____

Conclusion/Holding: _____
_____
_____
_____
_____

Vocab:	Questions:	☐ Upheld
		☐ Overturned
		☐ Questioned

Case: _____ Court: _____

Facts: _____
_____
_____
_____
_____

Issue: _____
_____

Rule: _____
_____
_____

Analysis: _____
_____
_____
_____
_____
_____
_____
_____
_____
_____
_____
_____

Conclusion/Holding: _____
_____
_____
_____
_____

Vocab:	Questions:	☐ Upheld
		☐ Overturned
		☐ Questioned

Case: _____ Court: _____

Facts: _____
_____
_____
_____
_____

Issue: _____
_____

Rule: _____
_____
_____

Analysis: _____
_____
_____
_____
_____
_____
_____
_____
_____
_____
_____
_____

Conclusion/Holding: _____
_____
_____
_____
_____

Vocab:	Questions:	☐ Upheld
		☐ Overturned
		☐ Questioned

Case: _____ Court: _____

Facts: _____
_____
_____
_____
_____

Issue: _____
_____
_____

Rule: _____
_____
_____

Analysis: _____
_____
_____
_____
_____
_____
_____
_____
_____
_____
_____

Conclusion/Holding: _____
_____
_____
_____
_____

Vocab:	Questions:	
		☐ Upheld
		☐ Overturned
		☐ Questioned

Case: _____ Court: _____

Facts: _____
_____
_____
_____
_____

Issue: _____
_____

Rule: _____
_____

Analysis: _____
_____
_____
_____
_____
_____
_____
_____
_____
_____
_____

Conclusion/Holding: _____
_____
_____
_____
_____

Vocab:	Questions:	☐ Upheld
		☐ Overturned
		☐ Questioned

Case: _____   Court: _____

Facts: _____
_____
_____
_____
_____

Issue: _____
_____

Rule: _____
_____

Analysis: _____
_____
_____
_____
_____
_____
_____
_____
_____
_____
_____
_____

Conclusion/Holding: _____
_____
_____
_____
_____

Vocab:	Questions:

☐ Upheld

☐ Overturned

☐ Questioned

Case: _____ Court: _____

Facts: _____
_____
_____
_____
_____

Issue: _____
_____
_____

Rule: _____
_____
_____

Analysis: _____
_____
_____
_____
_____
_____
_____
_____
_____
_____
_____
_____

Conclusion/Holding: _____
_____
_____
_____
_____

Vocab:	Questions:	☐ Upheld
		☐ Overturned
		☐ Questioned

Case: _____   Court: _____

Facts: _____
_____
_____
_____
_____

Issue: _____
_____
_____

Rule: _____
_____
_____
_____

Analysis: _____
_____
_____
_____
_____
_____
_____
_____
_____
_____
_____
_____
_____
_____
_____

Conclusion/Holding: _____
_____
_____
_____
_____

Vocab:	Questions:

☐ Upheld

☐ Overturned

☐ Questioned

Case: _____ Court: _____

Facts: _____
_____
_____
_____
_____

Issue: _____
_____
_____

Rule: _____
_____
_____

Analysis: _____
_____
_____
_____
_____
_____
_____
_____
_____
_____
_____
_____

Conclusion/Holding: _____
_____
_____
_____
_____

Vocab:	Questions:	
		☐ Upheld
		☐ Overturned
		☐ Questioned

Case: _____ Court: _____

Facts: _____
_____
_____
_____
_____

Issue: _____
_____
_____

Rule: _____
_____
_____

Analysis: _____
_____
_____
_____
_____
_____
_____
_____
_____
_____
_____

Conclusion/Holding: _____
_____
_____
_____

Vocab:	Questions:	☐ Upheld
		☐ Overturned
		☐ Questioned

Case: _____   Court: _____

Facts: _____
_____
_____
_____
_____

Issue: _____
_____

Rule: _____
_____

Analysis: _____
_____
_____
_____
_____
_____
_____
_____
_____
_____
_____

Conclusion/Holding: _____
_____
_____
_____

Vocab:	Questions:	
		☐ Upheld
		☐ Overturned
		☐ Questioned

Case: _____ Court: _____

Facts:
_____
_____
_____
_____
_____

Issue:
_____
_____

Rule:
_____
_____
_____

Analysis:
_____
_____
_____
_____
_____
_____
_____
_____
_____
_____
_____
_____

Conclusion/Holding:
_____
_____
_____
_____
_____

Vocab:	Questions:	
		☐ Upheld
		☐ Overturned
		☐ Questioned

Case: _____   Court: _____

Facts: _____
_____
_____
_____
_____

Issue: _____
_____
_____

Rule: _____
_____
_____

Analysis: _____
_____
_____
_____
_____
_____
_____
_____
_____
_____
_____

Conclusion/Holding: _____
_____
_____
_____

Vocab:	Questions:	☐ Upheld
		☐ Overturned
		☐ Questioned

Case: _____ Court: _____

Facts: _____
_____
_____
_____
_____

Issue: _____
_____
_____

Rule: _____
_____
_____

Analysis: _____
_____
_____
_____
_____
_____
_____
_____
_____
_____
_____
_____

Conclusion/Holding: _____
_____
_____
_____
_____

Vocab:	Questions:	
		☐ Upheld
		☐ Overturned
		☐ Questioned

Case: _____   Court: _____

Facts: _____
_____
_____
_____
_____

Issue: _____
_____
_____

Rule: _____
_____
_____

Analysis: _____
_____
_____
_____
_____
_____
_____
_____
_____
_____
_____
_____

Conclusion/Holding: _____
_____
_____
_____

Vocab:	Questions:	☐ Upheld
		☐ Overturned
		☐ Questioned

Case: _____   Court: _____

Facts: _____

_____

_____

_____

Issue: _____

_____

Rule: _____

_____

Analysis: _____

_____

_____

_____

_____

_____

_____

_____

_____

_____

_____

_____

Conclusion/Holding: _____

_____

_____

_____

Vocab:	Questions:	☐ Upheld
		☐ Overturned
		☐ Questioned

Case: _____ Court: _____

Facts: _____
_____
_____
_____
_____

Issue: _____
_____
_____

Rule: _____
_____
_____

Analysis: _____
_____
_____
_____
_____
_____
_____
_____
_____
_____
_____

Conclusion/Holding: _____
_____
_____
_____

Vocab:	Questions:	
		☐ Upheld
		☐ Overturned
		☐ Questioned

Case: _____   Court: _____

Facts:
_____
_____
_____
_____
_____

Issue:
_____
_____

Rule:
_____
_____

Analysis:
_____
_____
_____
_____
_____
_____
_____
_____
_____
_____
_____

Conclusion/Holding:
_____
_____
_____
_____

Vocab:	Questions:	
		☐ Upheld
		☐ Overturned
		☐ Questioned

Case: _____ Court: _____

Facts: _____
_____
_____
_____
_____

Issue: _____
_____
_____

Rule: _____
_____
_____

Analysis: _____
_____
_____
_____
_____
_____
_____
_____
_____
_____
_____
_____

Conclusion/Holding: _____
_____
_____
_____
_____

Vocab:	Questions:	☐ Upheld
		☐ Overturned
		☐ Questioned

Case: _____ Court: _____

Facts:
_____
_____
_____
_____
_____

Issue:
_____
_____

Rule:
_____
_____

Analysis:
_____
_____
_____
_____
_____
_____
_____
_____
_____
_____
_____

Conclusion/Holding:
_____
_____
_____
_____

Vocab:	Questions:	☐ Upheld
		☐ Overturned
		☐ Questioned

Case: _____ Court: _____

Facts: _____
_____
_____
_____
_____

Issue: _____
_____
_____

Rule: _____
_____
_____

Analysis: _____
_____
_____
_____
_____
_____
_____
_____
_____
_____
_____

Conclusion/Holding: _____
_____
_____
_____
_____

Vocab:	Questions:	☐ Upheld
		☐ Overturned
		☐ Questioned

Case: _____ Court: _____

Facts: _____
_____
_____
_____
_____

Issue: _____
_____

Rule: _____
_____
_____

Analysis: _____
_____
_____
_____
_____
_____
_____
_____
_____
_____
_____
_____

Conclusion/Holding: _____
_____
_____
_____
_____

Vocab:	Questions:	☐ Upheld
		☐ Overturned
		☐ Questioned

Case: _____ Court: _____

Facts:
_____
_____
_____
_____
_____

Issue:
_____
_____

Rule:
_____
_____

Analysis:
_____
_____
_____
_____
_____
_____
_____
_____
_____
_____

Conclusion/Holding:
_____
_____
_____
_____

Vocab:	Questions:	☐ Upheld
		☐ Overturned
		☐ Questioned

Case: _____ Court: _____

Facts: _____
_____
_____
_____
_____
_____

Issue: _____
_____
_____

Rule: _____
_____
_____

Analysis: _____
_____
_____
_____
_____
_____
_____
_____
_____
_____
_____
_____
_____

Conclusion/Holding: _____
_____
_____
_____
_____

Vocab:	Questions:	☐ Upheld
		☐ Overturned
		☐ Questioned

Case: _____ Court: _____

Facts: _____
_____
_____
_____
_____

Issue: _____
_____
_____

Rule: _____
_____
_____

Analysis: _____
_____
_____
_____
_____
_____
_____
_____
_____
_____
_____

Conclusion/Holding: _____
_____
_____
_____
_____

Vocab:	Questions:	
		☐ Upheld
		☐ Overturned
		☐ Questioned

Case: _____ Court: _____

Facts: _____
_____
_____
_____
_____

Issue: _____
_____

Rule: _____
_____
_____

Analysis: _____
_____
_____
_____
_____
_____
_____
_____
_____
_____
_____
_____

Conclusion/Holding: _____
_____
_____
_____
_____

Vocab:	Questions:	
		☐ Upheld
		☐ Overturned
		☐ Questioned

Case: _____ Court: _____

Facts:
_____
_____
_____
_____
_____

Issue:
_____
_____

Rule:
_____
_____

Analysis:
_____
_____
_____
_____
_____
_____
_____
_____
_____
_____
_____

Conclusion/Holding:
_____
_____
_____
_____

Vocab:	Questions:	☐ Upheld
		☐ Overturned
		☐ Questioned

Case: _____ Court: _____

Facts:
_____
_____
_____
_____

Issue:
_____
_____

Rule:
_____
_____

Analysis:
_____
_____
_____
_____
_____
_____
_____
_____
_____
_____

Conclusion/Holding:
_____
_____
_____
_____

Vocab:	Questions:	☐ Upheld
		☐ Overturned
		☐ Questioned

Case: _____ Court: _____

Facts:
_____
_____
_____
_____

Issue:
_____
_____

Rule:
_____
_____

Analysis:
_____
_____
_____
_____
_____
_____
_____
_____
_____
_____

Conclusion/Holding:
_____
_____
_____
_____

Vocab:	Questions:	☐ Upheld
		☐ Overturned
		☐ Questioned

Case: _____ Court: _____

Facts: _____
_____
_____
_____

Issue: _____
_____

Rule: _____
_____
_____

Analysis: _____
_____
_____
_____
_____
_____
_____
_____
_____
_____
_____
_____

Conclusion/Holding: _____
_____
_____
_____

Vocab:	Questions:

☐ Upheld

☐ Overturned

☐ Questioned

Case: _____ Court: _____

Facts: _____
_____
_____
_____
_____

Issue: _____
_____
_____

Rule: _____
_____
_____

Analysis: _____
_____
_____
_____
_____
_____
_____
_____
_____
_____

Conclusion/Holding: _____
_____
_____
_____
_____

Vocab:	Questions:	
		☐ Upheld
		☐ Overturned
		☐ Questioned

Case: _____ Court: _____

Facts: _____
_____
_____
_____

Issue: _____
_____

Rule: _____
_____
_____

Analysis: _____
_____
_____
_____
_____
_____
_____
_____
_____
_____
_____

Conclusion/Holding: _____
_____
_____
_____

Vocab:	Questions:	
		☐ Upheld
		☐ Overturned
		☐ Questioned

Case: _____ Court: _____

Facts: _____
_____
_____
_____
_____

Issue: _____
_____
_____

Rule: _____
_____

Analysis: _____
_____
_____
_____
_____
_____
_____
_____
_____
_____
_____
_____

Conclusion/Holding: _____
_____
_____
_____
_____

Vocab:	Questions:	☐ Upheld
		☐ Overturned
		☐ Questioned

Case: _____   Court: _____

Facts: _____
_____
_____
_____

Issue: _____
_____

Rule: _____
_____

Analysis: _____
_____
_____
_____
_____
_____
_____
_____
_____
_____

Conclusion/Holding: _____
_____
_____
_____

Vocab:	Questions:	☐ Upheld
		☐ Overturned
		☐ Questioned

Case: _____ Court: _____

Facts:

Issue:

Rule:

Analysis:

Conclusion/Holding:

Vocab:	Questions:	☐ Upheld
		☐ Overturned
		☐ Questioned

Case: _____   Court: _____

Facts:
_____
_____
_____
_____

Issue:
_____
_____

Rule:
_____
_____

Analysis:
_____
_____
_____
_____
_____
_____
_____
_____
_____
_____

Conclusion/Holding:
_____
_____
_____
_____

Vocab:	Questions:	
		☐ Upheld
		☐ Overturned
		☐ Questioned

Case: _____   Court: _____

Facts:
_____
_____
_____
_____

Issue:
_____
_____

Rule:
_____
_____

Analysis:
_____
_____
_____
_____
_____
_____
_____
_____
_____
_____

Conclusion/Holding:
_____
_____
_____
_____

Vocab:	Questions:	☐ Upheld
		☐ Overturned
		☐ Questioned

Case: _____ Court: _____

Facts:
_____
_____
_____
_____

Issue:
_____
_____

Rule:
_____
_____

Analysis:
_____
_____
_____
_____
_____
_____
_____
_____
_____
_____
_____

Conclusion/Holding:
_____
_____
_____
_____

Vocab:	Questions:

☐ Upheld

☐ Overturned

☐ Questioned

Case: _____ Court: _____

Facts:
_____
_____
_____
_____
_____

Issue:
_____
_____

Rule:
_____
_____

Analysis:
_____
_____
_____
_____
_____
_____
_____
_____
_____
_____
_____

Conclusion/Holding:
_____
_____
_____
_____

Vocab:	Questions:	
		☐ Upheld
		☐ Overturned
		☐ Questioned

Case: _____   Court: _____

Facts:
_____
_____
_____
_____
_____

Issue:
_____
_____

Rule:
_____
_____

Analysis:
_____
_____
_____
_____
_____
_____
_____
_____
_____
_____
_____

Conclusion/Holding:
_____
_____
_____
_____

Vocab:	Questions:	
		☐ Upheld
		☐ Overturned
		☐ Questioned

Case: _____ Court: _____

Facts:
_____
_____
_____
_____
_____

Issue:
_____
_____

Rule:
_____
_____

Analysis:
_____
_____
_____
_____
_____
_____
_____
_____
_____
_____
_____

Conclusion/Holding:
_____
_____
_____
_____

Vocab:	Questions:	
		☐ Upheld
		☐ Overturned
		☐ Questioned

Case: _____ Court: _____

Facts: _____
_____
_____
_____
_____

Issue: _____
_____

Rule: _____
_____
_____

Analysis: _____
_____
_____
_____
_____
_____
_____
_____
_____
_____
_____

Conclusion/Holding: _____
_____
_____
_____

Vocab:	Questions:	
		☐ Upheld
		☐ Overturned
		☐ Questioned

Case: _____ Court: _____

Facts: _____
_____
_____
_____
_____

Issue: _____
_____

Rule: _____
_____

Analysis: _____
_____
_____
_____
_____
_____
_____
_____
_____
_____
_____

Conclusion/Holding: _____
_____
_____
_____
_____

Vocab:	Questions:	☐ Upheld
		☐ Overturned
		☐ Questioned

Case: _____ Court: _____

Facts: _____
_____
_____
_____
_____

Issue: _____
_____
_____

Rule: _____
_____
_____

Analysis: _____
_____
_____
_____
_____
_____
_____
_____
_____
_____
_____

Conclusion/Holding: _____
_____
_____
_____
_____

Vocab:	Questions:	☐ Upheld
		☐ Overturned
		☐ Questioned

Case: _____ Court: _____

Facts:
_____
_____
_____
_____
_____

Issue:
_____
_____

Rule:
_____
_____

Analysis:
_____
_____
_____
_____
_____
_____
_____
_____
_____
_____
_____

Conclusion/Holding:
_____
_____
_____
_____
_____

Vocab:	Questions:	
		☐ Upheld
		☐ Overturned
		☐ Questioned

Case: _____ Court: _____

Facts:
_____
_____
_____
_____
_____

Issue:
_____
_____

Rule:
_____
_____

Analysis:
_____
_____
_____
_____
_____
_____
_____
_____
_____
_____
_____

Conclusion/Holding:
_____
_____
_____
_____

Vocab:	Questions:

☐ Upheld

☐ Overturned

☐ Questioned

Case: _____   Court: _____

Facts: _____
_____
_____
_____

Issue: _____
_____

Rule: _____
_____

Analysis: _____
_____
_____
_____
_____
_____
_____
_____
_____
_____
_____

Conclusion/Holding: _____
_____
_____
_____

Vocab:	Questions:	
		☐ Upheld
		☐ Overturned
		☐ Questioned

Case: _____   Court: _____

Facts: _____
_____
_____
_____
_____

Issue: _____
_____

Rule: _____
_____

Analysis: _____
_____
_____
_____
_____
_____
_____
_____
_____
_____

Conclusion/Holding: _____
_____
_____
_____

Vocab:	Questions:	☐ Upheld
		☐ Overturned
		☐ Questioned

Case: _____ Court: _____

Facts:
_____
_____
_____
_____
_____

Issue:
_____
_____

Rule:
_____
_____

Analysis:
_____
_____
_____
_____
_____
_____
_____
_____
_____
_____
_____

Conclusion/Holding:
_____
_____
_____
_____

Vocab:	Questions:

☐ Upheld

☐ Overturned

☐ Questioned

Case: _____ Court: _____

Facts: _____

_____

_____

_____

_____

Issue: _____

_____

Rule: _____

_____

Analysis: _____

_____

_____

_____

_____

_____

_____

_____

_____

_____

_____

Conclusion/Holding: _____

_____

_____

_____

Vocab:	Questions:	☐ Upheld
		☐ Overturned
		☐ Questioned

Case: _____ Court: _____

Facts: _____
_____
_____
_____
_____

Issue: _____
_____

Rule: _____
_____
_____

Analysis: _____
_____
_____
_____
_____
_____
_____
_____
_____
_____

Conclusion/Holding: _____
_____
_____
_____
_____

Vocab:	Questions:	☐ Upheld
		☐ Overturned
		☐ Questioned

Case: _____   Court: _____

Facts: _____
_____
_____
_____
_____

Issue: _____
_____
_____

Rule: _____
_____
_____

Analysis: _____
_____
_____
_____
_____
_____
_____
_____
_____
_____
_____

Conclusion/Holding: _____
_____
_____
_____
_____

Vocab:	Questions:	
		☐ Upheld
		☐ Overturned
		☐ Questioned

Case: _____ Court: _____

Facts: _____
_____
_____
_____
_____

Issue: _____
_____
_____

Rule: _____
_____
_____

Analysis: _____
_____
_____
_____
_____
_____
_____
_____
_____
_____
_____
_____

Conclusion/Holding: _____
_____
_____
_____
_____

Vocab:	Questions:	
		☐ Upheld
		☐ Overturned
		☐ Questioned

Case: _____   Court: _____

Facts: _____
_____
_____
_____
_____

Issue: _____
_____

Rule: _____
_____
_____

Analysis: _____
_____
_____
_____
_____
_____
_____
_____
_____
_____
_____

Conclusion/Holding: _____
_____
_____
_____

Vocab:	Questions:

☐ Upheld

☐ Overturned

☐ Questioned

Case: _____ Court: _____

Facts:
_____
_____
_____
_____
_____

Issue:
_____
_____

Rule:
_____
_____

Analysis:
_____
_____
_____
_____
_____
_____
_____
_____
_____
_____
_____

Conclusion/Holding:
_____
_____
_____
_____

Vocab:	Questions:	
		☐ Upheld
		☐ Overturned
		☐ Questioned

Case: _____ Court: _____

Facts: _____
_____
_____
_____
_____

Issue: _____
_____

Rule: _____
_____
_____

Analysis: _____
_____
_____
_____
_____
_____
_____
_____
_____
_____
_____
_____
_____

Conclusion/Holding: _____
_____
_____
_____
_____

Vocab:	Questions:	
		☐ Upheld
		☐ Overturned
		☐ Questioned

Made in the USA
Las Vegas, NV
03 September 2023

76989721R00116